HAPPINESS STREET

HAPPINESS STREET

Poems by
Olya Stoyanova

Translated by Katerina Stoykova

Accents Publishing • Lexington, Kentucky • 2025

Printed in the United States of America

Accents Publishing
Editor / Translator: Katerina Stoykova
Cover: "A Balloon Prospect from Above the Clouds" from *Airopaidia* by Thomas Baldwin (1786)

ISBN: 978-1-961127-10-4
First Edition

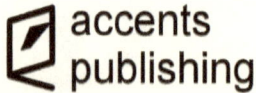

accents
publishing

Accents Publishing is an independent press for brilliant voices. For a catalog of current and upcoming titles, please visit us on the Web at

www.accents-publishing.com

CONTENTS

Approaching

Packing Luggage in Three and a Half Minutes / 3
Personal Experience / 4
Flea Market / 5
Instead of an Apology / 6
Happiness Street / 7
Small Stories / 8
Recipe / 9
About the Facts / 10
Good Morning / 11
Passing Through a Foreign City Early Morning / 12
A Tea House at 2500 Meters Above Sea Level / 13
A Reason to Go to the Beach / 14
Interior News / 15
People Should be Happy, / 16
Cultivating a Sense of Celebration / 17
The Chorus of Street Musicians / 18
Describing a Feeling / 19
The Woman from the Other End of the World / 20
Family Photo / 21
White / 22
An Idea / 23
The Silence / 24
Internal Relief / 25
Zen / 26

Small Moments

Monday Morning / 29
Peaceful Times / 30
Presence / 31
The New Masters / 32
Equilibrium / 33
A Lesson in Patience / 34
The Witnesses / 35
Symptoms / 36

Plans / 37
Family Story / 38
Still Life / 39
The Museum in Drama / 40
A Pigeon / 41
With Few Words / 42

Borrowed Landscapes

Autumn, 840 Meters Above Sea Level, Unexpectedly / 47
Road Market / 48
Dazhdovnitsa / 49
End of Story / 50
A House Next to the Station / 51
Bread / 52
The Story of Clouds / 53
Random Stops Along the Way / 54
Travel Guide / 55
Work Hours / 56
Archeology for Beginners / 57
Two Kids in the Entourage of the Great / 58
The Beginning of a Story / 59
In Prague at Noon / 60
Snapshot / 61
Landscape / 62
Bukhara / 63
Internal Directions / 64
Athens, Airport / 65
Night Shift at the End of the World / 66
A Church in a Small Tourist Town / 67
The Great Geographical Discoveries / 68

Acknowledgments / 69

About the Author / 71

About the Translator / 71

I know you are tired,
but come:
this is the way.

—Rumi

Approaching

PACKING LUGGAGE IN THREE AND A HALF MINUTES

Small crises,
deep scrapes,
earthquakes—
she stands, holding two bags,
having gathered everything
she considers vital
in the rush—
an old photo of her parents,
a couple of books,
a toy for the child,
a few pieces of clothing,
lots of chaos.
Everything she cannot do without,
everything
she can live with.

PERSONAL EXPERIENCE

Seeking
the right words—
like mushrooms—
some outright poisonous,
others—
even more unsuitable.

FLEA MARKET

Monday,
7pm.
A little red dress
is draped on the railing
of Luvov Bridge.
The dress's owner—
a woman of a certain age—
sits five meters away
and observes, with some detachment,
to see if there is interest
in her memories.
There isn't.

INSTEAD OF AN APOLOGY

Each morning—
on my way to work—
the old man,
sitting on the front steps
of the bank—
stretches out his hand and asks:
What time is it, child?
What can I tell him—
each morning
at the same time
it's late,
very late....

HAPPINESS STREET

On this street
there is only one house—
old
and so low
that one must bow
to enter.

SMALL STORIES

She likes to write notes—
"I love you" to her husband,
"I'm thinking of you" to her child,
"thank you" to her mother.
It's a little ludicrous actually,
but her loved ones don't speak of these things,
even pretend
they've never
discovered anything in their pockets.
Still, she's been doing this a while—
since the day
she read somewhere
that a woman jumped from the fourteenth floor,
and in her pocket, a note:
"five eggs and a loaf of bread."

RECIPE

Fatigue steadily accumulates.
It all starts quite early—
A spoonful for mommy,
a spoonful for daddy,
a spoonful for aunty
and more, and more.

ABOUT THE FACTS

In a neighborhood church
in Florence
several kids
slip among the tourists,
cause a commotion,
drop notes
in front of Beatriche's grave
and leave,
gesturing and laughing loudly.
"What's going on here?"
asks a man
who found
a place to sit
in this town
where no one stops.
"Nothing, nothing,"
the priest explains.—
"There is a legend that
whenever you feel heartache
you come here,
write a letter to Beatriche Portinari,
and she fulfills your plea."
They both keep silent,
and the man smirks:
"Yeah, sure, heartache...
        These children?!"
On his way out he reads a sign
that on this spot Dante first met
Beatriche.
Both were nine,
and he fell in love forever.

GOOD MORNING

One morning he wakes up
and has trouble recognizing
the man in the mirror—
another person stares back at him,
somewhat familiar,
a bit disappointed,
a man
who no longer dreams,
and on whose face is written:
a good husband,
conflict averse,
a father of three,
same as his father,
a copy of his grandfather.
This is simply a morning
like any other—
he smooths his hair with his fingers
and leaves.
The rest is clear.

PASSING THROUGH A FOREIGN CITY EARLY MORNING

that could
be her—
the woman
crossing on red
to catch the bus
and falling in the middle of the street;
the mother
leading her grown daughters
by their hands,
while they smile condescendingly
above her head;
the man
walking hesitantly
on a rope-bridge
as if taking his first steps
or the girl
smoking a cigarette
on the 12th floor balcony
and seeking out the silhouette of the moon.
And on and on.
And it's only morning.

A TEA HOUSE AT 2500 METERS ABOVE SEA LEVEL

The tea
doesn't matter.
The point is
that you arrive.

A REASON TO GO TO THE BEACH

With the passing of years
the bodies become laden—
a few folds
too many,
more bumps on the skin,
more stories,
varicose veins,
burst capillaries
and other,
otherwise invisible details.
The inconvenience of
complicated family relationships aside,
it's more impressive how
entire families get together
as if for the first time—
fathers and children,
grandmothers and uncles,
mothers and sons,
varicose veins
and gravity.

INTERIOR NEWS

She enjoys sensing
how conflicts ripen—
not international scandals
that make news,
or terrorist attacks
or crisis situations,
but the inconspicuous family sagas,
the small dramas reaching
their boiling point—
the man strides too heavily,
breathes loudly,
the children become uncontrollable,
and she feels how something inside her
starts to rebel—
extremely lightly,
exceptionally slowly …
This could turn
into a real revolution
she tells herself.—
I just have to give it
enough time
to ripen.

PEOPLE SHOULD BE HAPPY,

says a Buddhist lama
visiting from Amsterdam
for just one day.
The women are beautiful,
the sky is blue,
what's the problem,
he asks and smiles
with all his teeth.

CULTIVATING A SENSE OF CELEBRATION

Throughout the years he realizes
how holidays have stopped bringing him joy—
what's left
if you don't pick out presents
with excitement
and don't invest in small gestures—
it would be foolish to believe in Christmas
and justice in the world.
At thirty he thinks
he's aged and is frightened
that by sixty, for example,
he'd have just as much time
to accumulate knowledge
and sorrow, and to poison the holidays.

THE CHORUS OF STREET MUSICIANS

Dreary February
in Venice—
crowds in raincoats
and a string orchestra
hiding from the rain
without ceasing to play.
Five meters up the street Elvis Presley
invites a sparse crowd to rock-and-roll, baby,
and a little farther down
a Black musician leans on the wall
and plays the blues
for hours.
Gondoliers pass by him
and yell out to one another:
"Ciao Marco!"
"Ciao Michele!"
A small Japanese woman
first snaps a photo of him
then in a rush of goodwill
hands him a fistful of coins,
but he jumps:
"Thanks, ma'am!
But today I am a Venetian!"

DESCRIBING A FEELING

Patience is
kneading bread which is not
going to be enough.

THE WOMAN FROM THE OTHER END OF THE WORLD

Every summer
she crosses half a continent
to come here—
one more delight,
one more summer
before the end,
to sense once more
the eyes glued to her,
to warm up once more
in this vast sun,
to not think of wrinkles
and the cold seasons of old age.
… only one more summer,
and then I'll rest.

FAMILY PHOTO

She's twenty-two,
he—twenty-five.
They look as though
the photographer
is making them uncomfortable.
Perhaps they're holding hands
for the photo,
but that's not visible
in the frame.
Fifty years ago
people smiled
only with the corners of their mouths,
but there is nobody to read
these signs now.
The heirs have rented out
the house along with the portrait above the bed.
"What are we going to do with these two?"
asks one of the tenants,
and the rest have nothing to say.
Besides, what's the problem—
he's been gone fifteen years,
she—three.
The photo simply covers
a white stain on the wall.
Later the tenants wrestle
with shadows awhile until
finally, to hide the stain,
they slap on a landscape.
Perhaps Rome.
At least Rome is eternal.

WHITE

He knows
that when things fall apart,
they turn white.
The fatigue sneaks in
whenever two people
keep silent while
playing out conversations
in their heads,
each knowing
the retorts of the other.
Haven't you noticed how this happens—
every time winter arrives unnoticed
without colors,
with silence.

AN IDEA

Whenever he feels unhappy
he notices every detail—
how the smitten man
carefully hugs his plump wife,
how the child holds
her mother's hand,
how the dumb songs
the neighbor plays
incessantly repeat
my love,
my love.
He notices each gesture
of that man—
how he places his hands
on the wide midriff of his wife,
how she smiles
and leans her head to the side.
He sees how the child
insistently looks up, seeking
her mother's eyes,
as she stares straight ahead
and says:
"Come on,
hurry up, hurry up."
Then it occurs to him
that only a very sad God
could have created
all these details.
Because it seems as though
happy people need
much less.

THE SILENCE

The elderly man guarding the church
is already hard of hearing.
He perceives only whispers,
attempts to read lips
and worries somewhat—
that if one day
a voice tries to tell him something,
he might not hear.
And everything will continue
as usual.

INTERNAL RELIEF

He can name
each recess
of their common landscape,
knows the fearsome power
of the landslides
that originate inside him
and wipe out
ten years of shared life
with just one word.
He also knows
all the innocent abrasions,
the wrinkles
that accumulate slowly,
the invisible
subterranean fatigue.
He also knows
all the wounds and injuries,
navigates the roughness
of cohabitation
and is frightened
that such science
is yet to be invented.

ZEN

Quiet after the storm—
she's got nothing to say,
because in such moments
words gradually lose
their ability to hurt.
This is zen,
she insists.
Meaning—you don't give a damn.

Small Moments

MONDAY MORNING

Running late
on his way to work,
he jaywalks, and there,
on the median
a roar of a distant siren
catches up with him.
He looks around for
a fire, a tragedy, police,
so early on a Monday morning
when the world seems
a brittle and fragile place.
The scream of the siren
rubs against his legs like a dog,
and for a couple of seconds
he is able to distinguish
through the frosted windows
of the ambulance
the silhouettes of people
with their heads bowed.
Then everything ends suddenly –
the roar gradually dies out,
it's Monday again,
and he is standing on the median,
needing time to remember
who he is
and why the hurry.

PEACEFUL TIMES

In ancient Samarkand—
the city
still remembering
Genghis Khan and Timur—
a man sits at the market,
selling
pomegranates.

PRESENCE

Behind the altar—
a small lizard crawls out.

THE NEW MASTERS

Tunisians,
naked from the waist up,
sweaty and glossy like onyx,
joyfully whitewash
a XIII century chapel of St. Michael
at the French Riviera.
And they truly do good work.

EQUILIBRIUM

At two in the morning
he hasn't slept yet –
at that time
he doesn't feel like reading,
or sitting in front of the computer,
or listening to the radio.
He simply lies for another hour or two
in the dark
listening to the soft breathing next to him.
That calms him down.
Something like a mantra—
I am here
and that's where I need to be.

A LESSON IN PATIENCE

According to the travel guide, this is
The madrasa of 40 columns,
yet he counts them for the third time—
twenty pillars made of ebony,
stained by time,
carved with flowers
and smoothed by sand.
The others from the group are also
circling each other under the arches—
women, posing for photos
then absentmindedly touching
the rough sinews of the wood,
kids counting—one, two, three ... twenty.
And all over again.
The Mullah stands apart and smiles,
because to see
all forty columns
you don't need arithmetic
but patience—
twenty pillars before you
and twenty more
in the waters of the lake.
How come nobody has ever learned
this lesson.

THE WITNESSES

A boy and a girl
hold hands
at the mountain top
of Cannes castle.
Then the boy quicky sneaks a kiss
and looks around to check
if someone saw them.
Well,
someone did see them—
an entire busload of Russian tourists,
a few Romanians
and two Germans.
Some even took photos.
But that doesn't count.

SYMPTOMS

He's a surly person
yet gets emotional
over small things.
In one moment, he feels tenderness
about the well-maintained
roads in the woods.
Another time—
by the woman who gives names
to the frightened cats in the neighborhood.
He has no explanation
for these moments.
He thinks this is like
a toothache—
it hurts from too much sweetness.
And from good things.

PLANS

With time
he loses the ability
to create friendships—
doesn't know where exactly
to start the complicated knitting
of conversation,
misses the moments
when he is supposed to reinforce
what's already been said
and tie a knot
and most of all he doesn't believe
that something may come out
of all this, and that he could wear it
at least a season or two.

FAMILY STORY

Albums are filled
with old people
staring fiercely
at the camera
without blinking,
ears sticking out,
smoothed bangs,
and the kids ask
"are these bad people?"
"Why would they be bad!"
I say, though it's hard
to have your picture taken, knowing
that from that moment on
you become a photo
that someone will be touching
with chocolate fingers,
leaving prints
on the nose,
on the chin,
on the dignity
of years.

STILL LIFE

These apples
have been picked early in the morning.
When sins
and guards
are sound asleep.

THE MUSEUM IN DRAMA

A XIX century icon
in which an anonymous painter
has taken liberties—
The Virgin Mother firmly presses her son
to her cheek—
the way all mothers pose
with their kids in family photos.
It's not according to the canon—
says the monk apologetically.
But this Virgin Mother
is plumper and more beautiful.

A PIGEON

lands on the windowsill.
The mother,
who is measuring
her son's temperature,
interprets it
as a sign.

WITH FEW WORDS

Words are ailing—
sometimes for a while,
other times—a day or two,
and that's that.
At that point, he pays no attention
to who says what
but focuses on the small gestures—
how she hands him
a glass of water
in the morning
or how she combs his hair
with her fingers
before an important meeting.
Do I need to
explain?

Borrowed Landscapes

*The true story of a person is the story of
the wanderings of his attention.*

—José Ortega y Gasset

AUTUMN, 840 METERS ABOVE SEA LEVEL, UNEXPECTEDLY

Here the grass
hasn't burnt yet
and smells like regular
20 stotinki herbal tea.

ROAD MARKET

Afternoon, 36 degrees Celsius, Anatolia.
The grandmothers sitting cross-legged
next to the road,
hide in the shade,
heads covered,
arrange and rearrange
baskets of peaches and strawberries.
They yawn,
idly glancing at cars
whooshing past them,
and assess the world
simply and clearly—
some will go,
others will come,
there is always traffic.

DAZHDOVNITSA

Above the window
of an abandoned house—
a swallow's nest—
youthful shrieks at home again.

END OF STORY

In Samarkand
seven-year-old Ana
runs under the blue domes of the madrassas—
there
seven centuries ago
echoed the voices
of silk merchants
and the sighs
of zurna players—
and releases a kite.

A HOUSE NEXT TO THE STATION

From this point of view
the world is constantly moving
back and forth,
always departures
always arrivals,
and she—always at the same place—
lower
and lower.

BREAD

The woman
selling bread
at the market in Istanbul
doesn't yell,
doesn't bargain,
doesn't entice the crowds:
bread is like the sun—
early morning
it will rise on its own,
by evening
there will be nothing left.

THE STORY OF CLOUDS

Some time ago
she was able to decipher the sky—
the most detailed topographical map
of unfamiliar lands.
She discovered the blank areas of unfamiliar territories—
sharp peaks
and shifting sands,
managed to divine the shadows of an unfamiliar species of fish
that flew by in minutes
then morphed into something else
that pushed the story forward.
This map had no end.
Now it's a lot easier.
Stratocumulus.
Nimbostratus.
Altocumulus lenticularis.
The world is clear and predictable.
It will rain.
It won't rain.

RANDOM STOPS ALONG THE WAY

These houses
have no owners—
the doors are open, and inside
hang old wedding photos
of people
nobody remembers.
Anyone can enter
to drink water
(if they have the patience to wait
for the dark water to run out),
pick fruit from the trees
with branches weighed to the ground,
make a path
in the tall grass
and leave.
One can explore
all houses,
touch everything—
the dust, the sharp edges of a bed,
the spoons on the table,
and understand
that such houses exist,
and from that point on
only random travelers
will be their owners.

TRAVEL GUIDE

From afar
the city appears dirty—
the closer you get—
the more intense the taste.

WORK HOURS

Between one and three
the gates
of the church
are closed—
not that God
has work hours,
but the woman at the cash register
is human too.

ARCHEOLOGY FOR BEGINNERS

Open necropolis
by the sea
lizards crawl
and wild blackberries grow—
after fifteen centuries
what better proof
that everything
is dust and wind.

TWO KIDS IN THE ENTOURAGE OF THE GREAT

> Happy is the one
> who has forsaken the world
> before the world has forsaken him.

> —Headstone inscription at the Gur-e-Amir tomb, XIV century, Samarkand

Among the stones
marking the graves
of ancient military commanders
rest two miniature
jade headstones—
of two children—
two monarchs,
who didn't stain
their hands with blood.
From time to time
misguided tourists
bow to them.

THE BEGINNING OF A STORY

Mothers
hanging children's laundry
along the windows
of a hospital.

IN PRAGUE AT NOON

Each day for years
a miniaturist
has been painting on the grand plaza—
minding neither traffic,
nor the bell chiming,
nor the curiosity of tourists
who peek—
as if they can perceive in a moment
that which he's been drawing for months.
"Every person is inhabited
by two angels—
one good and one evil" he tells them.
"Where, where" the tourists ask;
he hands them a magnifying glass and
together they examine the miniatures.
"Right here"—he points.
The devil is in the details.
And the angel, also.

SNAPSHOT

The monastery
smells of strawberries.
Two men carry
trays of jam
and chase away the cat
that moseys
at their feet—
it's June,
it's high,
it's far.

LANDSCAPE

Flocks of ravens by Elbe—
late Fall,
naked branches
and low sky—
someone else will need to describe them.
I'm only passing through.

BUKHARA

Do you know
where is the ancient Bukhara,
Muslims' fourth holiest city
after Mecca, Medina and Jerusalem?
Here,
in Central Asia,
enclosed by desert
on three sides,
the city resembles a mirage—
madrasas and sand-colored
fortress walls,
people walking,
squinting against the wind,
and wind
that lifts women's dresses
very high.
They say
that's how cities survive.

INTERNAL DIRECTIONS

In a village up the mountain
two people sit next to one another
and look in different directions.
The woman—to the west.
The man—toward the high cliffs.
When the clouds hang heavy above,
their eyes meet.
"Look at what's coming our way," says the man.
And she turns.

ATHENS, AIRPORT

August afternoon, Wednesday—
among the boards with arrivals and departures,
among the signs
for duty-free shops
and restaurants and restrooms
with baby-changing stations—
a sign points towards a chapel—
somewhere on the second floor
right along the hallway,
at the very end.
There the crowds disappear
and another world begins—
one woman
slowly arranges candles,
props them up when they lean,
relights them when they go out,
maintaining the heavenly traffic.

NIGHT SHIFT AT THE END OF THE WORLD

A small gas station
on a minor road—
at two in the morning
a man stops
to buy chocolate and water.
        At four—a couple gets out
to stretch in the dark
and to exchange a few words with others.
        Later a family stops by
to casually ask—among other things—
if this is the right direction.
        At four fifteen—
Maria—the cashier
comes out for a breather
and sees the giant full moon
swaying over the dark hills.
It's the 15th of August,
thirty kilometers farther
the highway begins,
after ten more
the sea stretches
and she senses salt in the air.
        At fifteen to seven
a young woman stops
to get gas
and amiably asks:
"How are things here—
        at the end of the world?"
Maria is twenty-three
and already has an answer:
"In fifteen minutes
my shift is ending."

A CHURCH IN A SMALL TOURIST TOWN

In the church where
tourists constantly peek in
only one woman has come
to do work—
she's praying
in one of the chambers,
laboring to interpret
every sign other than
casual laughter
flashes of cameras
and the impression that
the world is full of
fortunate people.

THE GREAT GEOGRAPHICAL DISCOVERIES

A family
stops along the way—
lowers the car windows
and asks—
is there a road
ahead?

ACKNOWLEDGMENTS

Happiness Street was first published in Bulgarian by publishing house Janet 45 in 2013.

"Small Stories," "Instead of an Apology," "Recipe," "Zen" and "Passing Through a Foreign City Monday Morning" were included in *The Season of Delicate Hunger: Anthology of Contemporary Bulgarian Poetry* (Accents Publishing, 2014)

"Flea Market," "Family Photo," "Monday Morning" and "Bukhara" have previously appeared in the Bulgarian issue of *Body*.

ABOUT THE AUTHOR

Olya Stoyanova is a poet, writer and playwright based in Sofia, Bulgaria. She is interested in the relationship between poetry and science, nonfiction writing and social problems, dramaturgy and women's point of view. Olya is the author of five poetry collections, a novel, two short story collections and three nonfiction books. Her last poetry book, *Happiness Street*, won two national awards for the best poetry book of the year 2013: the Ivan Nikolov award and the Nikolay Kunchev award. She won the National Askeer Award for the Best Dramatic Text of the Year twice, in 2014 and 2018, for the plays *Invitation to Dinner* and *The Color of Deep Waters*. Her plays *Invitation to Dinner* (Sofia Theatre, 2014), *The Color of Deep Waters* (Ivan Vazov National Theatre, 2017), and *Fear of Taming* (Ivan Vazov National Theatre, 2020) are currently on stage.

Olya Stoyanova is the Editor in Chief at Bulgarian National Radio Network's Hristo Botev Channel for Culture, Science and Education, and a Lecturer in the Faculty of Journalism and Mass Communication at Sofia University.

oj@abv.bg

ABOUT THE TRANSLATOR

A Bulgarian by birth, Katerina Stoykova is a bilingual poet living in Kentucky and is the author of *Between a Bird Cage and a Bird House* (University Press of Kentucky, 2024) and *The Poet's Guide to Publishing: How to Conceive, Arrange, Edit, Publish and Market a Book of Poetry* (McFarland, 2024). Katerina is the founder and senior editor of Accents Publishing, as well as the creator of the *Accents* podcast on WUKY. Katerina served as the 2023–2024 Director of the Kentucky Book Festival, as well as the Director for the Center for the Book in Kentucky and is the 2025–2026 President of the Kentucky State Poetry Society.

www.ingramcontent.com/pod-product-compliance
Lightning Source LLC
Chambersburg PA
CBHW020806130626
46554CB00006B/2313